Overcoming Challenges of Autism in Kids

7 Effective Strategies Autism Parents Can Leverage for Successfully Raising an Autistic Kid

Frank Dixon

Before we begin, I have something special waiting for you. An action-packed 1 page printout with a few quick & easy tips taken from this book that you can start using today to become a better parent right now!

It's my gift to you, free of cost. Think of it as my way of saying thank you to you for purchasing this book.

Claim your download of Profoundly Positive Parenting with Frank Dixon by scanning the QR code below and join my mailing list.

Sign up below to grab your free copy, print it out and hang it on the fridge!

Sign Up By Scanning The QR Code With Your Phone's Camera To Be Redirected To A Page To Enter Your Email And Receive INSTANT Access To Your Download

ARE YOU BUSY?

LISTEN TO THE AUDIOBOOK

ANYTIME. ANYWHERE.

EXCLUSIVELY AVAILABLE ON audible

Give Audible a try!

Sign up by scanning the QR code with your phone's camera

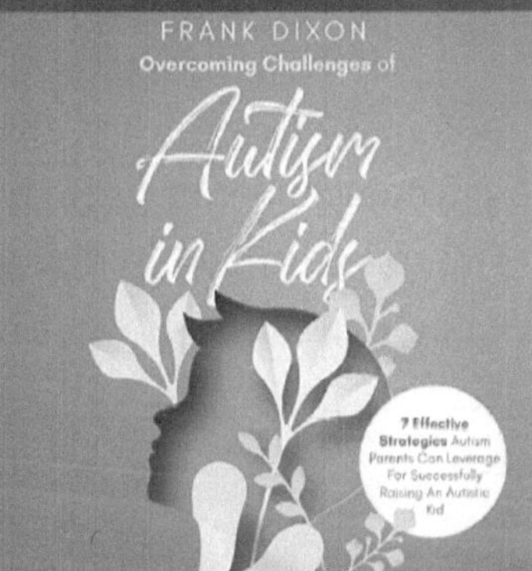

With Audible you can listen to this book and others like it

Regular offers include:

- Try Audible for $0.00
- Access a growing selection of included Audible Originals, audiobooks and podcasts.

Fully flexible:

- Email reminder before your trial ends.
- 30 day trial.
- Cancel anytime.

Before we jump in, I'd like to express my gratitude. I know this mustn't be the first book you came across and yet you still decided to give it a read. There are numerous courses and guides you could have picked instead that promise to make you an ideal and well-rounded parent while raising your children to be the best they can be.

But for some reason, mine stood out from the rest and this makes me the happiest person on the planet right now. If you stick with it, I promise this will be a worthwhile read.

In the pages that follow, you're going to learn the best parenting skills so that your child can grow to become the best version of themselves and in doing so experience a meaningful understanding of what it means to be an effective parent.

Notable Quotes About Parenting

"Children Must Be Taught How To Think, Not What To Think."

– Margaret Mead

"It's easier to build strong children than to fix broken men [or women]."

- Frederick Douglass

"Truly great friends are hard to find, difficult to leave, and impossible to forget."

– George Randolf

"Nothing in life is to be feared, it is only to be understood. Now is the time to understand more, so that we may fear less."

– Scientist Marie Curie

Table of Contents

Introduction

Being an autism parent is different from parenting other types of children. It's hard to say, as different parents go through unique challenges with their autistic children. Many grapple with uncertainty about the development and fear that their child will be left behind. Some fear that their child will require 24/7 support and care. Others worry about how the child will make it on their own once they pass away.

However, the way you perceive challenges and overcome them is tremendously important because it is what makes raising an autistic child joyous.

In most cases, a parent's biggest fear is how they can make their child with special needs feel less anxious in social settings. They want them to become a better communicator, improve self-regulation, and cope well in unpredictable circumstances. Many children with autism spectrum disorder (ASD) are startled by simple things such as loud noise, bright lights, or strange smells. Once that happens, their anxiety with the uncertainty takes over. It can end with a meltdown, self-harm practices, and even depression.

Since autism is a spectrum, the way the brain functions, perceives things, learns, and expresses itself varies from child to child. This also means that different children can have different triggers. Some symptoms are common, but most are different. These symptoms help doctors put the child at either of the three functional levels. Identifying your child's support needs, doctors can prescribe therapies to improve communication, behavior, and comprehension. For parents, understanding these levels prepares them to deal with the unique challenges that come with it.

ASD Level 1: Requiring Support

This is the mildest of ASD. It is also known as the most functioning form of autism. Children with level 1 ASD have trouble communicating with others appropriately. They face difficulty in reading social cues and body language. They can speak in full sentences but not engage in a back-and-forth dialogue with others. Children with ASD level 1 also have few friends. Toddlers have trouble moving from one activity to another. Their planning and organizational skills are poor which prevents them from leading an independent life like other children of their age do.

ASD Level 2: Requiring Substantial Support

These children have more trouble with verbal and social communication than children with ASD level 1. They have shorter attention spans and find it challenging to focus on one thing or move from one activity to another. Children with ASD level 2 have narrow interests, engage in repetitive behaviors, and have trouble functioning normally in uncertain situations. They can communicate but speak in simple and short sentences. They also do poorly with reading social and nonverbal cues.

ASD Level 3: Requiring Very Substantial Support

ASD level 3 is the most severe form of autism. The degree of the behaviors we talked about in ASD Level 1 and 2 becomes extreme. Children with ASD level 3 have trouble with expression, both verbal and nonverbal. This makes it challenging for them to function in most cases and interact with others. They also engage in repetitive behaviors and have short attention spans.

Learning about these signs can prepare them to make their child feel supported and loved. Apart from these levels, many symptoms are common in children with autism spectrum disorder. The most common symptoms in infants and toddlers include:

- Delayed speech development or no speech at all
- Rejecting touch like hugs and kisses initiated by others
- Preferring to play solo and paying little attention to what other children are playing
- Reacting negatively when told to do something

- Showing intolerance toward others entering their personal space
- Having no awareness of others' personal space
- Rarely using facial expressions and body gestures when communicating
- Playing with toys in an unimaginative and repetitive manner
- Disliking certain foods because of their taste, color, or texture
- Getting upset when something happens outside of routine
- Not responding when being called by their name
- Having unusual sensory interests like sniffing things or people

In older children and adults, symptoms are slightly different. For example, they may have the following:

- Avoid spoken language
- Have monotonous speech and prefer using pre-learned phrases
- Can't have a normal, two-way communication

- Talk at people instead of talking to them
- Take things literally, can't read sarcasm, and can't understand figures of speech
- Not comprehend certain basic social interactions

This book is written with these symptoms and challenges in mind. It serves as a guide to help parents who have recently learned of this condition and are at a loss on how to proceed with the diagnosis. Although autism isn't curable, children with this disorder can lead fulfilling and happy lives. With some care and support, they can improve their behaviors and reactions. They can adopt better communication and social skills. They can have successful and blooming careers in any field of interest as many famous people we know of with autism spectrum disorder. Let's learn how to overcome the challenges and raise successful and happy autistic children.

Chapter 1:

Autism and Its Many Colors

Autism spectrum disorder (ASD) is a developmental disability. The term autism is derived from the Greek word *autos* which means "alone." It causes significant social, behavioral, and communication deficits. Its symptoms appear before the age of three. As per research, boys are five times more likely to have ASD than girls. Statistics put 1 in 68 children at risk of developing ASD. There is no cure for ASD; however, with therapy, its symptoms can be controlled. There is no proof of how it develops and why some children have it and others don't (Centers for Disease Control and Prevention [CDC], 2014).

People with ASD may not look different from others, but their actions and poor communication skills set them apart. They can learn to communicate, behave, and interact better with various forms of therapies. As discussed previously, depending on the level of support they need, some people with ASD can lead normal lives independently, while others need help daily. Some famous people with ASD include:

- Tim Burton
- Steve Jobs
- Lewis Carroll
- Charles Darwin
- Bill Gates
- Vincent van Gogh
- Steven Spielberg
- Emily Dickinson
- Alfred Hitchcock
- Thomas Edison
- George Orwell
- Alexander Graham Bell
- Benjamin Franklin
- Henry Ford
- Satoshi Tajiri
- Michelangelo

- Carl Jung
- Lionel Messi
- Jane Austen
- Jerry Seinfeld
- Nikola Tesla

In this first chapter, we look at the many types of autism spectrum disorder and what each condition presents. Later, we learn of the many helpful therapies that can help improve the quality of life for children and adults with an autism spectrum disorder.

Understanding the unique challenges your child's condition presents, you can devise a plan to help them cope with it. So far, five major types of autism have been identified. These include:

Asperger's Syndrome

Asperger's syndrome is a mild type of autism spectrum. People with Asperger's are often diagnosed later in life. They have normal intelligence and communication skills; however, they may find social interactions hard to navigate. Some challenges for people with Asperger's syndrome include not being able to read nonverbal cues or misinterpret them. They find it hard to guess someone's thought process through their facial expressions, gestures, and body language. People with Asperger's syndrome are also hypersensitive to sensory input or stimuli. Another characteristic is limited but hyperfocused interests. Some famous people diagnosed with Asperger's syndrome include Albert Einstein, Susan Boyle, Sir Anthony Hopkins, and comedic actor Dan Aykroyd.

Pervasive Developmental Disorder—Not Otherwise Specified (PDD-NOS)

Sometimes referred to as atypical autism, this is a wide-ranging type of autism spectrum and involves individuals who lie somewhere in the middle of Asperger's syndrome and autistic disorder. The severity of the symptom is common. The most common feature includes delays in movement or speech. Due to this, people with this disorder have developmental delays and difficulties in social and communication skills. Jazz prodigy, Matt Savage, had PDD-NOS. He was a gifted being and highly talented. He recorded his first album at seven.

Autistic Disorder

People with autistic disorder have trouble communicating. They don't do well with eye contact. They won't respond when being called, have a flat pitch while speaking, have repetitive behaviors, and must have a stringent routine. You can say that they have an issue with fixation as well, as they become hyperfocused over a specific thing. People with autistic disorder also experience a heightened intolerance of sensory input.

Rett Syndrome

Rett syndrome is a rare and severe type of autism spectrum disorder. It is linked with a defect in chromosome X and affects females mostly. Some characteristic symptoms include slow regression in skills after a normal developmental period. People with Rett syndrome experience loss of communication skills and purposeful hand movements.

Childhood Disintegrative Disorder

Like Rett syndrome, this is also a rare type of disorder where one starts as a normal individual and then experiences regression in skills much later in life. Children with this disorder exhibit loss of skills across all developmental areas, such as language, motor, social, and behavioral.

Diagnosis and Treatment

Diagnosing ASD is difficult since there isn't a medical test to determine the cause and severity. Doctors review the developmental history of an individual to form a diagnosis. Since every child develops at a different pace, it is difficult to pinpoint whether their brain works differently or is just wired for other things better. For example, some children are quick learners when it comes to speaking words. Some are naturally shy, and despite knowing and understanding what they are being told, they don't verbally respond. Therefore, the earliest diagnosis can be confirmed after the child turns 18 months or more. By the time they turn two, there is a set of developmental milestones they should have reached. If not, the diagnosis is further considered reliable. However, since the condition can take different forms in different children, many don't receive a final diagnosis until later in life. The sooner we diagnose a child, the better. Delay in a confirmed diagnosis means that the child won't be given the help they need while growing up.

As stated earlier, since there is no cure for ASD, doctors can rely on various therapies and interventions to improve the quality of a child's life. The sooner a child begins therapy or intervention, the greater their chances of leading a quality life.

When we speak of therapies, there are many. It is easier to discuss them in broad categories than on their own. Ideally, any intervention or therapy for people with ASD should follow structure and be consistent, interdisciplinary, and intensive. When all these conditions are present, there is a higher chance for improvement in areas such as communication and behavior.

Behavioral Approaches

Applied Behavior Analysis (ABA)

Applied behavior analysis works on behavioral problems in children. It views behavior in three steps: instruction, behavior, and consequence. ABA uses rewards and reinforcement to encourage desired behaviors and motivate the learning of new skills. ABA techniques include:

- Discrete Trial Training: This method helps children master complex tasks by breaking them down into simpler subcomponents. The technique repeats the desired skills and behavior until the child learns to adopt them.

- Pivotal Response Training: It focuses on four important areas of child development, including self-management, motivation, self-initiation, and responsiveness when given cues.

- Early Intensive Behavioral Intervention: In this method, the goal is to minimize atypical behaviors of autism in younger children.

Standard Approaches

- Occupational Therapy: This type of therapy uses many strategies aimed at helping children with autism perform effectively in everyday tasks by focusing on developmental areas like gross motor and fine motor skills.

- Speech Therapy: Speech therapy helps people with communication problems. They use alternate methods like picture boards, gestures, and creative outlets like music to help children express their ideas and thoughts better.

- Sensory Integration Therapy: Sensory integration therapy helps children who get triggered by certain sounds or touches. This form of therapy allows them to take charge of their senses and be more conscious of their movements, emotions, and sounds. It improves social skills and reduces awkwardness.

How Does Autism Affect Children?

Others make a lot of speculation regarding children and adults with autism. For starters, they function normally like others in most cases. Having read about the many celebrities, leaders, and artists above, this should not come as a shock. It will surprise you that we did not diagnose many of these people with autism while alive. Jane Austen was one of them. It wasn't until a century after her death that it was speculated that she might have suffered from Asperger's syndrome. Lionel Messi, for example, is one of those people you would never think to be on the autistic spectrum because he is one of the top players of this time, playing at his best in every game.

So, if they all act normal and look the same, how can you assume one child has autism, and the other doesn't?

Science tells us that autistic children may not reach the same developmental milestones as their peers when they should. Science also tells us that autistic children exhibit loss of previously developed social and language skills. To help comprehend, imagine this: A two-year-old child loves to play games of make-believe. A four-year-old child loves to play with other children in the park. An autistic child may not do either of the two because they have trouble interacting and socializing with others. They also have difficulty doing well in simple games like make-believe.

Then, autistic children also engage in repetitive behaviors. They can give their parents or caregivers a hard time with bedtime and compulsively eat non-food items like paper, chalk, sand, or Styrofoam. They may have meltdowns when something happens out of their schedule, like a guest coming over uninvited when they are supposed to go out to play. They find it hard to thrive in an unpredictable environment.

Chapter 2:

Educate Yourself and Others

Hearing a doctor tell you that your doubts were, in fact, accurate observations is both satisfying and sinking. At first, you feel happy that you were right to seek professional help, and then, that brief moment of joy is overshadowed by a long and heartbreaking thought—you were right. You knew there was something wrong with your child!

The diagnosis can feel like a punch in the gut for any parent or caregiver. You experience losing all hope, as you realize that there is no cure for autism. You imagine how life would change for you, your family, and your child; how they will not enjoy the same activities and blessings in life as you did; and how they will miss out on great friends and meaningful relationships with a partner all because they have trouble communicating and interacting with others.

But this is untrue. Sure, the diagnosis will change a few things, but it shouldn't change the way you see your child. The condition isn't the only thing that defines them. They are much more than that.

However, the first step is education—education for you, your family, educators, and everyone they meet with, including their peers, relatives, and neighbors. Many parents who receive the diagnosis are at a loss at how to move past it. They aren't mentally and emotionally prepared to take on the role of a consistent caregiver in their child's life. They worry about their other relationships and roles. They are a partner, a parent to their other children, a co-worker, and a friend.

If you are one of those parents that have just received a diagnosis, know that you are not alone. All the feelings you have been experiencing are normal. There may not be any cure for ASD, but there is always hope. As long as you hold on tight and don't let your child be discriminated against because of their pervasive developmental disability, you will be fine. As long as you don't let your fear and grief take over and take away your emotional and mental peace, you will be fine. As long as you don't think that the disability will take away your child's happiness and right to have all the good things in life, you will be fine.

The first step is to educate yourself and others around you. You can research and reach out for help to gain better insights on how you are going to do about the diagnosis. Before that, you must prepare yourself mentally and emotionally because chances are, this is going to be a long fight, and you need to be armored for it.

After the Diagnosis: Becoming Mentally Prepared

A diagnosis doesn't change the fact that your child can still accomplish whatever they set their heart on. With research exponentially growing over the past decades, there is always some new information or treatment idea worth trying. Many institutions have also played a key role in helping parents come to terms with the diagnosis by starting support groups and sharing their stories online. Many schools and colleges have also encouraged teachers and children to become aware of the condition and be more sensitive and attentive toward those who have it. Many hospitals now offer effective programs and interventions for children to improve communication; gross and fine motor skills; and vocational training to help young ones lead healthy, happy, and productive lives.

Yet, being their primary caregiver, what role you play still has the most merit. The sooner you research therapies and start interventions, the better. The more you speak about the disability with others and educate them to be compassionate, patient, and supportive, the higher the chances that these uniquely different children will feel more welcome and motivated. Here's how you can do this by mentally preparing yourself.

You can't let the diagnosis intimidate you. Allow yourself and your partner to realize. Pick books that answer questions about how to change your daily lives to help children with autism. Speak to different therapists, educators, and experts in the field to be guided better. Soon, you will look back on this day and feel happy about the sane and necessary choices you made without getting intimidated.

You can't allow the diagnosis to make you feel sorry for yourself. This isn't the end of the world for you or your child. Things could have been much worse. So many parents would wish to change places with you today—parents who lost their children to a miscarriage, stillbirth, or worse, children that battled cancers or heart defects early on. Learn to count your blessings.

Don't let the diagnosis make you forget who they are. Don't look at your child differently. They are still the same. You fell in love with them when you first met them. Don't let the diagnosis take away that memory from you. Some parents become so fearful of the future for their children that they forget to make the most of the present. Right now, what's most important is your kindness, empathy, and compassion.

There will be times when your child will have a meltdown, and you will get a lot of stares from strangers. Don't take that to heart. Don't listen to them when they tell you to discipline your child. Don't feel judged by those stares because you know that discipline, in this case, will be pointless. Instead, feel confident in your approach to dealing with the meltdown. Don't let some uneducated stranger school you or humiliate you.

Also, don't forget about the love and attention your other children need and deserve. Give them your time and affection, too. Deal with the diagnosis as a family. Speak to them about how things are going to change a little and how appreciative you will be if they can offer support. Reassure them you don't love them any less, and make time for them, too.

You shouldn't allow autism to take away your happiness and sense of humor, either. Decide: You can choose to be bitter and dwell on the what-ifs all day and night, or you could accept what is and make the most of the time you have with your child. You can't let the diagnosis suck the fun out of your life.

Remember: There is always hope. You can't allow the diagnosis to see your child differently or hope for a different future. They can still go to school, excel in their academics, learn to drive, get a job, plan a wedding, and have kids. Life doesn't end here for your child. Sure, some things will become more challenging than before, but look on the bright side: If all these things may not be happy, then modify your expectations of them.

Use your energy and time wisely. There is no point getting into frivolous debates that pull away from your attention and waste your time. How you want to proceed with the diagnosis, when it is the right time to tell everyone, and if you should label your child as an autistic child are all up to you. You have the right to decide what is best for your family and your child.

Don't get bothered by what others think or say. Steer clear of all negativity.

Get Help and Research

It isn't uncommon for parents who have just received a diagnosis of ASD to blame themselves or each other's family. Some mothers believe it is because they didn't stop drinking a glass of wine before knowing they were pregnant. Some fathers think that just because they have someone in the family with a similar disorder, they have passed it down to their child. It will shock you that some partners believe it is because they worked at a chemical or pharmaceutical company. All this has nothing to do with your child's ASD. It isn't your fault or anyone's fault. You could have done everything differently and still be presented with the same diagnosis. It doesn't matter if you were strict or permissive with your child or how much you cuddled or loved your child—there is no connection.

Even today, scientists are struggling to present solid evidence as to what causes it, whether environmental, social, economic, and medical factors play a role or not. If there is something you can control and be sure about, it is this: What you will do next!

ASD, with the right information, is a manageable disability. With the right information, you can educate yourself and others, make wise decisions, and choose the best mode of therapy for your child. This makes seeking the right information even more important. Rely on trustworthy sources like government and hospital sites that quote studies with references. Also, know that a child with autism does not differ from a child with bad habits. They do not differ from someone that chews loudly, bites pull the hairs of others, or has no sense of someone's personal space. A child with autism may have trouble sitting calmly in one spot, have attention deficits, or become agitated about every small thing. If you can counter chewing loud or hitting others with some strategic tactics, you can increase sensory input as well.

Reach out for support and don't become isolated. Seek help and read about the stories of other autism parents. Take inspiration from how they deal with the daily challenges and take things slow. Find adults with autism and ask them for tips and instructions. Contact people who have walked a few miles in your shoes. Thanks to online forums, you can reach out to people across the globe and feel you are in the same boat. It will always make it easier to navigate when two people are grappling with the same troubles.

Many local support groups offer more knowledge and emotional support for parents with an autistic child. It can be a great place to start and garner some support. You can also look up national charities that promote recreational workshops and interventions from time to time for autistic children and their parents.

Last, remember that things may seem hard at the moment, but they will only get better now that you have a confirmed diagnosis. You and your child are still the same people as before. The disability doesn't change a thing.

Autistic people deserve all the things any other child deserves, and they should get them.

Chapter 3:

Stick To a Routine

Routines become the bedrock of our daily lives. We know what they expect us to do upon waking up. This knowledge sets the pace and mood for everything else that follows. Uncertainty makes us fearful. We don't feel prepared for it. It pressurizes us, scares us, and bothers us. However, we aren't a fan of predictability either. It appears boring, monotonous, and well expected. There is no room for some element of spark. There is no excitement. It's like reliving the same day every day.

Yet routines are important for children with ASD. They need consistency, and they need everything. Routines and structures keep things from getting complex. They reduce stress and prevent them from having a meltdown over something as small as more cereal in their milk than required. Consistency establishes order. It keeps them calm and fosters an opportunity for a happy, shared family time. It's a win-win for everyone in the house, especially you.

Research has long-rooted the importance of structure and routine in children's lives. There is only so much that they know about, and new information, when presented chaotically, can feel threatening. Studies reveal that children who follow a daily routine have a 47% increased likelihood of improved social-emotional health than those who don't (Muñiz et al., 2014).

Routines, for children, do more than just prepare them for their day ahead. They also eliminate any power struggles that happen because of them. They help maintain quiet in the house when things go as planned. The structure also fosters cooperation because there are clear expectations set earlier. There is little to no confusion about what's expected of the child and what the child expects in return. This allows parents to limit any temper tantrums and misbehavior in children and nurtures a positive, strong, and healthy parent-child relationship. Most importantly, routines and structure allow children to take ownership of their activities—something that is highly important for children with autism. Feeling empowered and confident to navigate through the challenges daily life presents them with fosters independence and self-reliance.

Consistency Plays a Key Role

According to Reena Naami, director and owner of Spark Center for Autism, the schedules and consistency in routines go a long way for children with autism. She believes that a lack of routines can be the difference between success and failure for an autistic child. Her experience, knowledge, and interaction with many children and parents have compelled her to say that children who don't have a schedule may see delays in progress. She also believes it is an important reason for regression sometimes, where a child forgets what they learned earlier (Spark Center for Autism, 2019).

The more consistent one is with scheduling and structure, the more they can work on areas that an autistic child finds troubling. For example, if a child struggles with a poor attention span or has speech problems, a routine and schedule that involves daily activities and promotes honing both skills can prove beneficial in the long run. By engaging them in activities that require attention, you can prevent a lack of focus.

Many times, when working on a certain behavior trait, parents see a spike in that behavior instead of a reduction in it. This means that the therapy or learning isn't consistent or appropriate for the child.

With communication deficits and the inability to express themselves freely, it can become hard for parents to communicate with their children. Being consistent in the ways we handle daily nuisances makes it easier for both the parent and the child. For example, your child may misbehave when fed by a caregiver instead of you, especially if they expect you to do it.

Children with autism also have challenges adjusting to any unnecessary or unexplained changes in their routine. Parents must ensure to keep a track of time to prevent any meltdowns. Unexplained changes in their routine will make them question everything else in their life because they like to create a pattern of thought that follows the next. For example, if they wear a green shirt daily, and today, you ask them to wear a red shirt instead, it changes everything. They have to rethink every scenario in their head, reimagine all the pictures in their head, and go through with the change. You can imagine the amount of stress they will be in. You can expect an increase in their challenging behaviors if you cannot keep up with a consistent routine and structure.

You can avoid power struggles by ensuring that you two are on the same page with expectations. The transitions can turn smooth if both parties are aware of what's expected. For this, you must identify the things that set them off and notice how they respond to those triggers. Do they resort to physical aggression, like throwing things around or harming themselves? Or do they become agitated, anxious, or all sweaty? How they respond to inconsistency will help you find strategies to combat the reactions. Second, you must communicate how you feel about those reactions with the child. Does it anger you? Do you feel sad or judged? Does it make you feel like a negligent parent? Some children, old enough to understand, will empathize in return and try to behave better. If they have poor vocal skills, you can use body language and gestures to make them understand your concern.

As soon as you establish an effective channel of communication, you can give yourself and your child some time to self-reflect. Together, you can devise a plan that works well for you. However, the goal should remain consistent and so should the rewards and reinforcement that follow. Once both parties understand each other's situation better, they can work as a team as opposed to one another.

Last, consistency and routines will also reinforce learning of the desired behavior and action.

Establishing Routines: Starting Right

A resistance to change is the primary cause of the many challenges children with autism face. A daily routine can serve as a powerful tool in helping them deal with the uncertainty that it leads to.

Knowing what behaviors will end with rewards and compliments will decrease destructive behaviors. Routines give children with ASD a safe space to return to when adapting to new situations. Many autistic children have issues with completing a certain task but are excited about completing another. However, since all tasks are equally important, routines teach children they will have to make peace with an unwanted task too before moving on to a preferred task. For instance, they must know that a reward will only be achievable if they finish homework first.

To encourage this, they should have a say in what they would like to do, how to do it, and when. For example, taking a bath is important—even if it appears as an uninteresting activity. Autistic children have increased sensory input, and they don't like being touched. The idea of a bath, therefore, is not the most exciting to them. However, since it is imperative, you can give them the choice to decide when they would like to take one. Including them in the decision-making process will make them feel empowered and validated. It will also minimize any ill-disciplinary behavior. You can brief the child about what they must do and instruct them on how to do it. For example, they will need to remove clothing before getting into the bathtub.

Setting expectations in such a manner will reduce confusion as well. It will bring them some security, as they can plan out things in their mind beforehand. This also goes well with establishing other tasks like eating, playing, doing homework, and bedtime, etc.

Often, the demands and circumstances cause them to interrupt a child's routine. Children with ASD are quick to notice and protest the change by using undesirable behaviors like yelling, self-inflicted injury, verbal or physical attacks, and other destructive behaviors. When this happens, let the child know that their actions, whether positive or negative, will have certain consequences. Be consistent with those consequences so that autistic children can reduce negative behaviors, as positive consequences don't follow them up. Once your child gives up undesirable behavior, return to the routine.

You can also look up to the technique called priming. Priming allows parents to give autistic children a preview of situations they may struggle with before they happen. This sets in some predictability and reduces unexpected reactions. Social stories are a form of priming. They let your child know what's about to happen and mentally prepare them for it. For example, if you have a visit to the doctor coming up, start reminding your child about it a day or two before its date. You can talk about what they would like to wear, when would be the right time for them to visit, what plans should you make after the visit like eating out or going to a park, etc. Be specific and only make promises you can keep. You can also share pictures of how the hospital looks like, the doctor or a simple procedure, and what it entails. Setting expectations in such a manner cuts down on any surprises that trigger anxiety. It also reassures the child that the experience will be a positive one.

You can also make use of calendars and timetables. You can mark important dates and events so that your child knows what to expect and when. You can also create vision boards about an important event like your sister's wedding or your child's birthday party.

Timers also come in handy here because autistic children often have trouble switching from one activity to another. Setting a timer before the activity lets them know they will have to give up and move on to another one once the buzzer goes off.

Whichever technique or strategy you use, start with small changes. For example, if you want your child to have their lunch after changing their school outfit, don't be too insistent if the child wants to have lunch first. You can simply remove their shoes and socks or tie at first, and once the child is comfortable with it, you can remove their pants and shirt—of course, with their permission first.

Chapter 4:

Positive Reinforcements Go a Long Way

Children on the autism spectrum face behavioral challenges throughout their lives. Childhood is especially difficult, as they are just learning about new things and trying to communicate. Several studies suggest positive reinforcements prove effective in this case (Hardy & McLeod, 2020; Schuetze et al., 2017). It is as effective as discipline is, for non-autistic children. When we use discipline, the goal is to eliminate unwanted behaviors. With positive reinforcements, although the goal is the same, the strategies used don't include the concept of punishments. Positive reinforcements include rewards, both tangible and intangible, when the desired behavior occurs.

Positive reinforcement is the basis of applied behavior analysis (ABA), a technique commonly used by therapists to improve the quality of life for children with ASD. A child that complies with the request for positive behavior receives an incentive. Repeated incentives form a habit and help the child limit misbehavior. This is what ABA techniques focus on.

To increase positive behaviors and reduce negative ones, we set rewards for children with autism.

For children, positive reinforcements, feedback, and encouragement go a long way in motivating and disciplining them. It is truer for children with ASD. Well-timed and well-thought rewards and compliments make them gain control of their actions and behaviors. They also build confidence and promote healthy behavior adoption.

As parents, we are quick to point out negative behaviors and punish our children for them. What we fail to monitor and appreciate are positive behaviors. Positive actions, no matter how small, should be acknowledged and rewarded.

Reinforcement happens when we reward a child for exhibiting a positive behavior to increase its likelihood. The reason positive reinforcements are effective is that children feel validated. They realize that doing well also pays off.. They realize their parents aren't blind to the good things they do. It is common to see toddlers using positive actions to get their parent's attention and appreciation.

With positive reinforcers, every parent can have a different idea. You may choose to reward some behaviors with tangible rewards and others with just praise. You can also decide when you want to use them. Timing, with positive reinforcements, is everything. A reward or compliment should come right after the desired behavior or else, they lose the knowledge. They fail to comprehend why they are being rewarded.

Positive reinforcement is effective when you realize the reinforcers that work best for your child. It is effective when you have chosen what behaviors you want them to demonstrate and stop focusing on the negative ones.

Choosing Positive Reinforcers

Positive reinforcers underline typical human behavior. We all love to be complimented and showered with gifts. Children love it even more because to them, gifts and compliments are more than just a gesture. It shows them that someone cares for them and loves them. When we know a reward is set, we modify our methods to attain it. When our boss promises us a promotion in the next quarter, our productivity and motivation increase. We put in more effort and work on efficiency. Positive reinforcements shape our behaviors, aspirations, and motivation. When we have an end goal in mind, all our efforts become directed toward it. The same happens for children with ASD. However, we must keep in mind that only appropriate reinforcers will work for our children. Every child responds differently to different things.

So how can we choose the right positive reinforcers? Is there a trick to it?

For starters, look for the things that have worked for them as reinforcers in the past. If the positive reinforcer doesn't excite the child, it will hold no value. It will certainly not motivate them to repeat the desired behavior. The first important tip is to find something that your child is passionate about. It doesn't have to be a tangible thing. It can also be an extra 15 minutes of their favorite cartoon before dinner. Keep in mind that, even though hugs and a pat on the back will reinforce, an autistic child might find them aversive. Recall a gift or gesture that worked for them in the past and start with that.

If you are still unsure, let the child decide the reward. Of course, there will be some limitations, but let the child tell you what they will appreciate.

You can also look at their deprivation state and decide what will serve well as a reward. For example, if the child has helped you set the table, you can cook a favorite side dish of theirs and have them eat it. You can also fulfill a need, like taking your child to ride their bicycle in the neighborhood because they appear bored.

Be sure to make the positive reinforcer practical and valid. Ideally, the reinforcer should be linked to the behavior or skill you are trying to encourage. Natural reinforcers occur anyway if the child engaged in a desired behavior or act.

Putting to Practice

Now that we are aware of what a positive reinforcer may look like, this last section lists some ideas to get started. Again, this is just a list of suggestions. Depending on what your child loves, you can DIY your rewards and use them as reinforcement.

Preferred Activity

A positive reinforcer can mean more time spent doing something your child loves. It can be watching TV, painting, or gardening. Emphasize why you are giving them extra time so that it may increase the likelihood of repeating the same behavior.

Verbal Praise

Verbal praise is another effective strategy. Simple sentences like, "I am so proud of you," "You did good," or "I knew you could do that!" are examples of sentences you can begin with. Verbal praise goes a long way, as children don't forget it soon.

Special Treats

If your child loves food-related activities, giving them special treats can work wonders as well. It doesn't have to be anything grand. It can be an extra cookie or an additional topping on their favorite ice cream to remind them they did well.

Toys

If affordable, toys make for amazing rewards and some memorable times. You can take them to the store and allow them to pick a toy of their liking to bring home with them. That is surely going to make them more motivated.

Privileges and Tokens

If you want to get more creative with your reinforcements, you can DIY special badges and tokens that they can use later. Tokens can list activities like a trip to the park or zoo. A badge can have something like "pride of performance" written on it, and they can wear it to school.

Chapter 5:

Provide a Stress-Free Space

Living with an autistic child in the house can be stressful. There is so much to take care of. From ensuring that lights aren't too bright, or the music played by the neighbors isn't too loud, you have to be vigilant at all times. Since children with autism have increased sensory output, it's difficult to keep them calm and anxiety-free. Although there is only so much that you can control in their lives, starting with an environment that is conducive to their comfort can be helpful.

Your house is the one place your child spends most of their time. If they like to stay indoors, as unpredictability in the outer world scares them, you ensure that their sensory needs are taken care of. Give them an environment where they can be themselves without worrying about what might happen and what might not keep them engaged and stress-free. It also eliminates the chances of any misbehavior and meltdowns. A lot of parents don't know how to make their homes more hospitable for their children with ASD. Unknowingly, they allow certain things and situations to happen that trigger anxiety in their children.

In this chapter, we look at how parents can make their home an ideal place for an autistic child by looking out for situations that cause stress and avoiding them.

Making Your Home an Inviting Place

You can begin by designating them a safe space to call their own. It can be their bedroom or play area in the lounge where they can play with their toys. Designating a separate spot in the house will make them feel safer and more comfortable when they are in that space and promote more regulated behavior.

Second, you need to work on eliminating triggers that cause agitation or anxiety. Since different children with autism get triggered by different things, you must make a note of what triggers your child and how you can avoid being in that situation. For example, let your friends and family know that they can't come uninvited to the house because it causes anxiety for your child. You can ask the mailman and delivery people to not ring the bell by placing a sign beside it stating how the sound startles your child. This way, you can look out for any pending frustration.

Similarly, some children with autism don't do well in social groups and like to play alone. They have a hard time with sharing their toys and become aggressive and agitated when told to. You shouldn't force your child to do either when you know it triggers their anxiety. You can start with other forms of therapies first and then gradually introduce them to people their age and encourage shared play.

You must also keep routines and schedules as consistent as possible. As discussed earlier, routines and structure alleviate uncertainty and boost self-confidence. The goal is to allow your child to be themselves and express themselves through their words and actions as much as possible. Routines can help establish that.

You must also pay attention to how you act around your overly sensitive child. Your actions and words should be confidence-boosting ones. They should uplift and encourage your child. Using positive language in the house leads to the development of healthy habits. This means not only that you speak to your child positively but also to your partner and other children.

To create a safe environment, you must also limit the number of distractions you expose your child to. Distractions take away focus; it is a known fact that many autistic children find focusing challenging. Therefore, if they are engaged in an activity and you wish for them to remain engaged, try to minimize any distractions that may take away their attention.

Providing Autistic Children a Calming Environment

A safe and calm environment also provides children with ASD a learning space for growth. They can experience calmness, build social skills, and improve speech and communication. This is possible when you declutter your house (or at least the space they own to themselves). Clutter promotes anxiety—even in normal children. Too much clutter can cause your child to feel claustrophobic. More stuff also equals more distractions. In some children, it can also foster unhealthy eating habits and trigger respiratory issues. Messy spaces cause autistic children to become easily overwhelmed.

To remove clutter, start with one room at a time and organize it. Keep the furniture and accessories to a minimum to avoid confusion and distractions. Get rid of things your child doesn't need or has used for a long time. This includes any books, toys, clothes, and fashion accessories they don't wear any longer. If your child has a strong connection with them, store them away in a safe place.

Put away items that can inflict self-harm. This includes all objects with sharp edges and items like glassware that can be used as well. These items can become a potential safety risk if your child resorts to physical aggression.

The next thing you need to do is minimize sensory overstimulation. Repair any noisy appliances, limit their usage when your child is at home, and hang blackout curtains in spaces that are prone to bright lights. Get rid of any cleaning products that come with a sharp scent, as that too can serve as a trigger. Children with autism display oversensitivity to such stimuli.

Designate a meditation or distraction-free spot in the house, and call it the quiet zone. This should be the space where the children can retreat when they feel anxious. No one but the child should be allowed to be in that space. Ideally, it should be somewhere that entertains minimum interruptions, like an attic or outhouse. Every time your child feels overwhelmed, they can head there and clear their head.

If you haven't disclosed to your extended family and friends about your child's diagnosis, do it at the earliest to avoid any surprise visits to the house uninvited. When children with ASD are expected to interact socially without prior notice, it can trigger their anxiety. The more a child feels pressured to mingle, the more stressed they will become. If your child struggles with holding a conversation, making eye contact, or being around people, be honest about it with others. Your child's mental and emotional health should be your priority.

Discuss methods to cope with stress and anxiety. Look up therapies that help minimize negative behaviors and meltdowns and incorporate them into your child's routine. There are many therapy activities that you can easily initiate at home without the need for a professional. For example, deep breathing exercises, yoga, and meditation can prove effective in calming the child. You can also teach your child to count when they feel anxious, as it distracts the mind from the immediate threat and calms the nerves. They can also go to their quiet zone and let go of their feelings in a healthy way.

Chapter 6:

Pay Attention to Triggers

Anxiety is a common problem for children with ASD. Although not every child may experience it severely, there need to be measures taken to reduce it as much as possible. Anxiety can manifest in many ways. Mostly, a trigger sets it off.

Despite promising advances in the area, understanding how to culminate it is limited. As different children can exhibit different symptoms, it is hard to abide by any set strategies that guarantee a quick remedy for a meltdown. Understanding more about the factors that trigger it is the first step toward prevention and culmination. We can counter anxiety by identifying the triggers that cause it and safeguard the child from being exposed to them.

According to one small-scale study published in the journal *Autism*, researchers held five focus groups involving parents of children and adolescents with anxiety disorders. The goal was to identify triggers, cognitive processes associated with anxiety, and behavioral signs (Ozsivadjian et al., 2012). Seventeen mothers had children with diagnosed ASD. Nineteen children had received ASD diagnoses from their local clinical services and suffered through severe levels of anxiety that impacted their everyday quality of life.

Common Triggers That Set off Anxiety

Although no two children will show the same level of anxiety, some behaviors common to children with ASD can cause a meltdown. A trigger can be a person, place, or thing where your autistic child feels threatened or uneasy. When in their presence, it can set off that loss of behavioral control. But parents can stave off the situation by becoming aware of what acts as a trigger and removing it from their child's path beforehand. Eileen Bailey, co-author of *The Essential Guide to Asperger's Syndrome* (2012), talks about these common triggers that set off fear in the child's minds about their safety and security. When they feel threatened, they resort to undesirable behaviors like yelling, pacing back and forth through the room, rocking in their chair, or throwing things.

Sensory Overstimulation

Sensory overload is a common trigger for children with autism. These children are sensitive to the sensory stimulation around them, like a crowded event, bright lights, loud music, or too much activity at once around them. It can make things stressful for them, as it becomes difficult to focus on just one.

Emotions

Experiencing fear, sadness, sorrow, or anger can also shape a child's behavior and actions. Houses, where unhealthy relationship patterns can be seen, can also lead to anxiety. If the child witnesses a fight among parents, a health or financial crisis, a home move, or the death of someone, it can make it challenging for them to cope with everything on their own. Children can sense the tension in the air and take it out on themselves. You can notice them appear quieter than before or become aggressive over trivial things. These indicate that there is some mental and emotional stress that the child is experiencing.

Changes in Routine or Structure

Children with autism crave structure in their lives. They like to have things predetermined for them. A lack of routine sets off unpredictability which can be scary. It leaves the child wondering what mode of defense mechanism they should resort to. Creating routines and setting expectations right from the beginning can reduce the number of meltdowns that happen in the house. Sudden plan changes, unannounced visits by guests, or cancelation of a trip that they were looking forward to are examples of triggers that can set off a meltdown.

Communication and Speech Difficulties

For children who have trouble with self-expression, having to converse with others can put them in a tough spot. For a nonverbal child, the frustration of not being able to express themselves can trigger a meltdown. The same goes for children with limited verbal skills.

Information Overload

Children with autism have trouble with focus and concentration. They get distracted easily because of a poor attention span. When there is an information overload, where the information they are receiving is too much or coming in at a fast speed, it can overwhelm them. Many children with ASD have delayed information processing, so they need more time than others to process each piece of information.

Coordination Issues

Coordination problems can also trigger stress and lead to a meltdown. Think about being chosen last for a play by people you call your "friends"—the ideas are hurtful. This happens often with children with ASD, as they suffer from good coordination. Their gross and fine motor skills aren't as polished as their peers. They can also have difficulty buttoning their shirt, unzipping their parents, wearing socks, or tying their laces. This causes tremendous stress, as they notice everyone else around them does it smoothly and in seconds.

Sensitivity to Food

Children with autism don't do well with surprises and therefore, are hesitant about trying new things. They have a list of favorites with food. They like to stick with food whose texture, taste, and smell they are familiar with. Being told to try something new for a change can be stressful. You can avoid a meltdown by sticking with the foods they know of and like and eliminating any food triggers that cause anxiety.

Hunger or Fatigue

Hunger and fatigue can also set off a meltdown. When the child is tired or hungry, they can act out in undesirable ways. If we deprive them of a good night's sleep, it can make them crankier than before. Similarly, if we leave them hungry for too long, it can irritate them. Again, this comes down to having strict routines and structure in their lives where things happen when they expect them to happen.

Culminating the Meltdown

When a meltdown happens, it is equally stressful for a parent. They have a few minutes to calm the child, especially when they are in public. Most meltdowns happen in mainstream places like a school, in the car, or a park where the child is grappled with uncertainty and wishes for the entire world to bend down to them. It is easy to think that you are trained to handle any challenging behavior that comes your way, but when the time comes to play your part, many parents freak out. However, the right strategies can go a long way in helping children with autism carry themselves better and practice emotional regulation.

Knowing that a meltdown could lurk just around the corner can add an extra level of stress to every situation. Once an autistic child has hit that meltdown, it's difficult for them to gain control again quickly. Thus, early identification, in this case, is the best cure. For this, keep a journal where you take notes on the many triggers that cause anxiety. This can be a great way to identify triggers and prevent future ones. As soon as you notice the first signs of a meltdown, you can devise a strategy to calm your child down and de-escalate the situation. Once you understand the triggers and the cause behind them, you can go in prepared and address the issues right away.

You must avoid surprises as well. Predictability keeps children with ASD relaxed. It is what makes them certain of the surrounding things. They feel safe when they know things are about to happen. To prevent any surprises, you can create charts and calendars that list different activities and events that the child is expected to deal with. You can create a chart for a week or a month and highlight their day-to-day routines specifically. Doing so will enable the child beforehand to prepare themselves in advance. You can also use timers and reminders if your child finds it challenging to move from one activity to another.

You can use visual prompts as well. Visuals are an excellent way of mapping out a situation. You can use it to explain things that are about to happen, such as guests visiting you. You can create a vision board or timetable where you use pictures and descriptions of what they can expect to happen to feel more empowered. They can feel better knowing what's about to happen. Vision boards are easy to create and make for an amazing and fun activity for you and your child.

Exercise of light to moderate level can also help a child during or after a meltdown. Exercise makes our brain release dopamine and limits the production of serotonin, the stress hormone. Dopamine helps calm the nervous system and promotes happy thoughts. If your child is talented at a sport, spend more time playing it. You can also play catch or just head out for a walk to calm the nerves.

You can listen to calming melodies and music together. When children with autism have a meltdown, music can do the same for their nervous system as exercise. It can nurture feelings of affection, comfort, and relaxation. Put noise-canceling headphones on your child when they are having a difficult time with a situation, and have them listen to some calming sounds like the sound of rain in a forest, water from a stream running down a hill, or a violin being played.

Chapter 7:

Celebrate Quirks and Talents

Parents of autistic children have unique struggles to deal with. Some days, it may seem like the struggles never end. There are so many things to be cautious about, from preventing meltdowns to ensuring a healthy and growing environment. It can soon become overwhelming. There are days when your child can't seem to be happy about anything, making you question your parenting style. They leave you wondering if it will get easier as they grow old or if your responsibilities only increase.

Being lost in such thoughts can make you forget about your child as being special. You get so worked up about their safety that you have little time to focus on who they are—apart from the disability.

Every child is a gifted child. They all have different quirks and talents. They each have different strengths and weaknesses. Strengths and weaknesses aren't always physical. Some children are excellent in academics, while others depict more expertise in playing sports.

Some have God-given vocals that can touch your heartstrings while others have a knack for playing musical instruments.

You would think that a child with a developmental ability won't have any special talents and skills since they have trouble with expression and speech, but this is where you are wrong. Children with autism or any other form of disability have special talents that can set them apart from the rest of their peers. As parents, we get so occupied with treating the condition and making sure our child feels safe that we don't notice that their disability isn't what makes them special. It is their many unique talents and skills.

Delivering praise and a chance to hone their talents and become an expert is also an important aspect of raising a child with autism. Knowing that they are good at something and then having an opportunity to become better can prove effective in shaping constructive behaviors and actions. Delivering praise also increases the likelihood of good behaviors sticking with them. This also promises a healthy parent-child relationship where the child feels appreciated and valued—not just a burden.

Celebrating Talents

Strengths represent areas of the highest functionality. If you are passionate about something, chances are, you will be good at it, too. The more time you spend honing that strength, the better you will get. We already know that being autistic doesn't hinder your child's ability to become successful. We know of the many artists and celebrities that made it big despite being on the autism spectrum. Providing young children with autism a chance to work on their strengths and focus on positive aspects of their personality can make them positive and motivated about setting prime goals for themselves. Recognition and encouragement of their talents can reinforce positive behaviors and keep them engaged in constructive activities.

But how can you do that? How can you show your child that you appreciate and recognize their skills and talents?

You start by focusing on how good they are. When you notice them doing something they love doing, compliment that behavior. Reinforcement is the key here. Instead of focusing on what behaviors they must let go of, you are focusing on what behaviors they should exhibit more of. This change of approach determines the difference between positive and negative behavior. If the child feels criticized all the time, they may lose interest in being good. They feel like nothing they ever do will be good enough for their parents. This starts a chain of negative thoughts, and the cycle can soon become vicious. Focusing on the strengths instead of weaknesses will therefore promote positive communication and make the child feel valued and appreciated.

Next, do more of the things they love. Invest more time and effort into activities they enjoy doing. For example, if they are into arts and crafts, there are tons of activities that they can engage in, like drawing, sketching, painting, and making DIYs. You can further categorize what sort of DIY they are interested in; for example, they can be into making jewelry, knitting wool, or making abstract art using paints. Similarly, if they are into gardening, activities like going to pick plants, planting seeds, and watering them every day, etc. are activities they might find exciting. The more time they spend doing something they love, the lower the chances of misbehavior and loss of emotional control.

You can also provide them with opportunities for growth by easing their path to success. For example, if they are good at a sport or musical instrument, you can set them up with a mentor to give them classes. If they are good at baking goods, you can enroll them in a weekend class on baking basics. You can also spend more time watching cooking shows or self-bake videos on YouTube and bake a cake together. If they are exceptionally good at singing, you can get them a karaoke machine or a microphone set as a present so that they can improve and become an expert. These are all ideas that suggest how you can celebrate their special quirks and talents by supporting them and providing them a chance to excel.

Delivering Praise

There is a right and wrong way to deliver praise and celebrate your child's unique talents and skills. Children with autism aren't as equipped with effective speech and communication skills. Therefore, you must keep the praise simple. You must use words they understand the meaning of. Using words that are difficult to comprehend can confuse them further and take away the essence of genuine praise.

You want to keep sentences short and smooth. Don't jumble multiple praises in a single sentence. Children with ASD experience a delay in processing information. Piecing it all together will make it harder for them to understand or remember. For a non-neurotypical child, it would seem appropriate to piece multiple praises together, but it's not for someone with autism.

Be consistent in how you praise. It might seem strange at first, but once you realize how they don't do well with surprises or change, you will want to keep your style of complimenting and reinforcement consistent. Autistic children have difficulty interpreting social cues. They may not view hugging as affection but as an invasion of their personal space. Similarly, they might not be too comfortable being patted on the back or kissed on the cheek without permission. Children with autism engage in repetitive behaviors. They will watch the same movies, listen to the same song, and do the same activity repeatedly without getting bored.

Therefore, keep that in mind when you go praising them. Be consistent with your praise and words when you compliment them on a repeated behavior.

Be specific with your praise, too. If you want to encourage a particular behavior, make sure that the child understands what they are being praised for. If you appreciate they brushed their teeth on time, make sure that you tell your child exactly that. It also prevents confusion and encourages the probability of repetition of the desired behavior. When being specific, be descriptive as well. For example, if your child brushes their teeth well, you can say something like this, "Great job at brushing your teeth. I see you reached every nook and cranny of your mouth."

Your praise should also sound authentic and genuine. Autistic children may not be the greatest deciphers of emotions behind actions, but they can sense when they are being complimented genuinely or not. Your praise should cling to their hearts in the warmest of ways. It should feel like you delivered it straight from your heart.

Praise should also come right away after the desired action. Earlier, we discussed the importance of positive reinforcement coming right after. Praise should also follow the desired behavior. Immediate feedback feels good and supportive. It shows the other person whose actions were noticed. It makes them feel validated. Besides, if you wait long enough for appreciation, the child will forget what positive action is being praised for.

Chapter 8:

Work on Improving Communication Skills

Communication is an exchange—an exchange of ideas, thoughts, needs, feelings, and desires. We may speak different languages, but being able to express ourselves and our ideas connects us all. Communication can also happen through written material. One core challenge with autism is the persistent exertion with social communication and interaction.

This isn't the case with all children but with most children suffering from autism. For some, speech is disordered, underdeveloped, or delayed. Some have trouble understanding language and holding a conversation, while others face problems with confidently expressing themselves. Usually, a lack of proper communication and speech is the first indicator that a child has autism.

Communication includes the comprehension of nonverbal behaviors as well as eye contact and body language. You can say a lot about a person by the way they carry themselves. If they have their hands crossed, don't maintain steady eye contact, or keep looking behind the person they are conversing with, it indicates a lack of confidence. Similarly, people who use their hands and arms with confidence appear to be experts on what they are talking about. A frown can show sadness, a smile depicts happiness, and grunting as anger.

Many preschoolers reach their speech milestones which is one reason autism can go undetected in many children at a young age. Since preschoolers don't talk as fluently and rarely understand the concept of sarcasm and jokes, it becomes difficult for parents to understand if there is something wrong with their child. Since every child grows at a different rate, speech and communication problems aren't detected until the child starts school and has to communicate more. Problems arise when they have to initiate and maintain a conversation, make friends, and take part in team activities.

Luckily, with the right strategies and therapies, speech and communication problems can be overcome in children and adults. They may not become as fluent and smooth as others their age, but you can expect to see a drastic improvement, provided intervention and therapies start early.

Common Speech and Behavior Problems

Your child may exhibit distinct problems than another child with autism. However, some common characteristics are visible in all. For example, children with ASD speak in either high-pitched or sing-song voices that fall flat and are robot-like. Bill Gates suffers from this trait—he has a flat tone and robot-like voice. Children with ASD also recite lines from a cartoon or movie verbatim. They can also talk endlessly about their favorite topics, often irrelevant to the conversation one is having. They don't understand or do well with slang. Repetition is another common trait where a child keeps repeating the same phrase again and again, like asking questions they already know the answer to or counting from one to ten without pause.

Another noticeable characteristic is echolalia where the child echoes what someone said or asked them. They repeat the same question as a response or develop stock phrases. Children with autism can also develop a strong vocabulary for something they are interested in yet cannot grasp the basics about another topic that doesn't interest them. Some children with high-functioning autism, like Asperger's, find themselves frustrated when they can't express themselves appropriately. They also feel humiliated and agitated when met with laughter and blank stares because they see it as rudeness. However, not everyone is trying to make fun of them intentionally. It happens because they have difficulty deciphering physical gestures and facial expressions.

They feel frustrated when they can't find the right words for their ideas and communicate them to another person. Children with autism also don't do well with social cues like they wouldn't understand why they shouldn't talk loudly at a funeral or remain quiet when eating dinner. They don't understand that others interpret such behaviors as disrespectful.

Children with autism also lack empathy sometimes. They can't view things from someone else's perspective or put themselves in another person's shoes.

Best Strategies to Promote Effective Communication

Children with autism can compensate for social communication through the learning of techniques and rules that foster better social interactions. They can take part in different treatment programs that specifically target improving social communication through speech-language learning.

Speech-learning therapy is a kind of therapy that focuses not only on correct pronunciation but also on back-and-forth communication and intonation. These aspects of pragmatic speech help children become better communicators and feel more confident about social events. Speech-language therapy engages the patients in role-playing exercises that promote collaboration, self-expression, and sharing. Other than speech-language therapy, different strategies can come in handy when the goal is to improve communication and social skills among children. These include:

- Picture exchange communication system (PECS)
- Communication boards
- Sign language

Conclusion

There is so much misleading information out there that makes us question our parenting skills. Some experts and websites vouch for giving children full freedom to be themselves, whereas others staunchly support keeping a tight hold of the reins to not make them take things for granted and do as they like.

Raising children in a polarized world is stressful. Raising an autistic child is a sure struggle. There are so many trials and challenges that come with this unique spectrum of conditions. Some children face issues with communication and speech where they find it challenging to express themselves effectively while others struggle with social interactions. They feel at a loss when it comes to making friends, working as a team player, and sharing things with others.

Children on the autistic spectrum have a hard time navigating social cues as well. They can't read or decipher sarcasm, have trouble maintaining eye contact, and don't do well when multiple ideas are pitched at them at once. They want a simple way of life where there is predictability and certainty. They aren't a fan of change and become anxious when they encounter it.

For a parent, this can be equally difficult. From getting a confirmed diagnosis about their child's condition to making the said changes in their lifestyle and routine, the journey is a difficult one. However, it can also be rewarding when the focus shifts away from the disability and onto the strengths and quirks of the child. By using positive reinforcements, praise, and appreciation, parents can raise happy and self-regulated children, ready to be on their own.

Thank you for giving this book a read. I hope you loved reading it as much as I enjoyed writing it. It would make me the happiest person on earth if you would take a moment to leave an honest review. All you have to do is visit the site where you purchased this book: It's that simple! The review doesn't have to be a full-fledged paragraph; a few words will do. Your few words will help others decide if this is what they should be reading as well. Thank you in advance, and best of luck with your parenting adventures. Every moment is a joyous one with a child.

References

7 autism behavior and communication strategies. (2021, September 23). National University. https://www.nu.edu/resources/7-autism-behavior-and-communication-strategies/

Autism 101: What everyone should know about it. (2018, November 24). Otsimo. https://otsimo.com/en/autism-treatments-facts-types/

Autism communication strategies that work. (n.d.). The Spectrum. https://thespectrum.org.au/autism-strategy/autism-strategy-communication/

Autism, PDD-NOS & asperger's fact sheets | using positive reinforcement for behavior management of children with asperger's syndrome or autism. (2019). Autism-Help.org. http://www.autism-help.org/behavior-positive-reinforcement-autism.htm

Bailey, E. & Montgomery, R. (2012, June 5). *The Essential Guide to Asperger's Syndrome*. Penguin Random House.

Carter, K. (2019, February 22). *How to make your home a stress free place for those with autism*. Jaden's Voice. https://jadensvoice.org/make-home-stress-free-place-autism/

Changing routines: Children and teenagers with autism spectrum disorder. (2020, November 18). Raising Children Network. https://raisingchildren.net.au/autism/behaviour/understanding-behaviour/changing-routines-asd

Centers for Disease Control and Prevention [CDC]. (2014, March 27). *CDC estimates 1 in 68 children has been identified with autism spectrum disorder*. CDC Newsroom. https://www.cdc.gov/media/releases/2014/p0327-autism-spectrum-disorder.html

Cherney, K., & Seladi-Schulman, J. (2021, November 3). *Everything you want to know about autism spectrum disorder (ASD)*. Healthline. https://www.healthline.com/health/autism#support

Clark, C. (2019, June 26). *Consistency is critical for kids with autism*. Detroit and Ann Arbor Metro Parent. https://www.metroparent.com/sponsored-content/consistency-is-critical-for-kids-with-autism/

Foundation, W. S. (2016, September 23). *Autism spectrum disorder*. White Swan Foundation. https://www.whiteswanfoundation.org/disorders/neurodevelopmental-disorders/autism-spectrum-disorder

Hardy, J. K., & McLeod, R. H. (2020). Using positive reinforcement with young children. *Beyond Behavior*, *29*(2), 107429562091572. https://doi.org/10.1177/1074295620915724

Hunt, A. (2020, June 10). *What is autism? Everything you need to know about the spectrum disorder*. GoodtoKnow.

https://www.goodto.com/family/what-is-autism-symptoms-and-diagnosis-110278

Jungle, S. N. (2021, September 3). *Six top tips for managing meltdown triggers for autistic pupils in school.* Special Needs Jungle. https://www.specialneedsjungle.com/six-top-tips-managing-meltdown-triggers-autistic-school/

Martinez, J. B. (2020, October 14). *My child was diagnosed with autism. now what?* Britannica for Parents. https://parents.britannica.com/my-child-was-diagnosed-with-autism-now-what/

Morin, A. (2021, June 23). *The most effective ways to discipline a child with autism*. Verywell Family. https://www.verywellfamily.com/discipline-strategies-for-children-with-autism-4005045#control-their-environment

Muñiz, E. I., Silver, E. J., & Stein, R. E. K. (2014). Family routines and social-emotional school readiness among preschool-age children. *Journal of Developmental & Behavioral Pediatrics*, *35*(2), 93–

99. https://doi.org/10.1097/dbp.0000000000000021

Newly diagnosed with autism | interactive autism network. (n.d.). Iancommunity.org. https://iancommunity.org/cs/newly_diagnosed

Newly diagnosed with autism: Things to help. (2019, May 2). Nhs.uk. https://www.nhs.uk/conditions/autism/newly-diagnosed/

Ozsivadjian, A., Knott, F., & Magiati, I. (2012). Parent and child perspectives on the nature of anxiety in children and young people with autism spectrum disorders: A focus group study. *Autism : The International Journal of Research and Practice*, *16*(2), 107–121. https://doi.org/10.1177/1362361311431703

Positive reinforcement | toddler ASD. (n.d.). Asdtoddler.fpg.unc.edu. Retrieved December 3, 2021, from https://asdtoddler.fpg.unc.edu/reinforcement/i

mplementation-steps/positive-reinforcement.html

Positive reinforcement and autism. (2021, February 24). Hidden Talents ABA. https://hiddentalentsaba.com/positive-reinforcement-autism/

Roy, H. (2018, May 10). *Catch them being good: The power of praise.* Autism Society of NC. https://www.autismsociety-nc.org/power-of-praise/

Rudy, L. J. (2010). *Why your autistic child can speak but can't communicate.* Verywell Health. https://www.verywellhealth.com/speech-vs-communication-260566

Rudy, L. J. (2018). *Making sense of the 3 levels of autism.* Verywell Health. https://www.verywellhealth.com/what-are-the-three-levels-of-autism-260233

Rules of engagement for praising a child with autism. (2015, March 30). Childrens Therapy TEAM. https://www.childrenstherapyteam.com/index.

php/2015/03/30/rules-of-engagement-for-praising-child/

Schuetze, M., Rohr, C. S., Dewey, D., McCrimmon, A., & Bray, S. (2017). Reinforcement learning in autism spectrum disorder. *Frontiers in Psychology, 8.* https://doi.org/10.3389/fpsyg.2017.02035

Smith, L. (2016, February 16). *The do's & don'ts after an autism diagnosis.* Autism Speaks. https://www.autismspeaks.org/blog/dos-donts-after-autism-diagnosis

Soffrin, A. (2017, May 5). *7 things to do when your child has an autism diagnosis*. Healthline. https://www.healthline.com/health/expert-tips-for-when-your-child-has-autism#Remember:-You-cant-change-your-child

Spark Center for Autism. (2019). *Meet the Spark Team!* Spark Center for Autism. https://www.sparkcenterforautism.com/meet-our-team/

The importance of consistency in caregivers of autism patients in a hospital setting. (n.d.). Special-Learning.com. Retrieved December 2, 2021, from https://www.special-learning.com/article/The_Importance_of_Consistency_in_Caregivers_of_Autism_Patients_in_a_Hospital_Setting

Understanding meltdown triggers in children with autism. (2018, April 9). Www.healthymepa.com. https://www.healthymepa.com/2018/04/09/understanding-meltdown-triggers-children-autism/

Using effective reinforcement strategies at home. (2018, August 24). The Place for Children with Autism. https://theplaceforchildrenwithautism.com/autism-blog/using-effective-reinforcement-strategies-at-home

wikiHow. (2014, September 12). *Raise an autistic child.* WikiHow; WikiHow. https://www.wikihow.com/Raise-an-Autistic-Child

Wilkinson, L. A. (2018, June 3). *Triggers for anxiety in autistic children*. Best Practice Autism. https://bestpracticeautism.blogspot.com/2012/09/autism-and-nature-of-anxiety.html

www.ingramcontent.com/pod-product-compliance
Lightning Source LLC
La Vergne TN
LVHW051018080826
845145LV00009B/2686

* 9 7 8 1 9 5 6 0 1 8 3 0 1 *